At the Bandstand!

A Rock 'n' Roll Review

Featuring Popular Music Arranged for 2-Part Voices
by Sally K. Albrecht, Jay Althouse, Andy Beck, and Greg Gilpin

With Original Material by Andy Beck and Brian Fisher

Recording Orchestrated by Tim Hayden

100% Reproducible! Staging Suggestions Included!

See back cover for CD Track Numbers.
Performance time: approximately 35 minutes.
Note: Reproducible Student Pages and color cover art are included
as PDF files on the Enhanced SoundTrax CD.

© 2013 Alfred Music Publishing Co., Inc.
All Rights Reserved. Printed in USA.

Book & CD (39961)   ISBN 10: 0-7390-9629-X   ISBN 13: 978-0-7390-9629-1
Teacher's Handbook (39959) ISBN 10: 0-7390-9628-1   ISBN 13: 978-0-7390-9628-4
Enhanced SoundTrax CD (39960)

NOTE: The purchase of this book carries with it the right to photocopy the entire book.
Limited to one school/organization. NOT FOR RESALE.

Alfred Cares. Contents printed on 100% recycled paper.

Cast of Characters and Costumes

*Rockin' Robin: — Flashy '50s TV host. Anchors the show with charm and charisma. Wears a slick retro-style suit.

*Cindy Sullivan: — The kind-hearted "girl next door" type, in a cute '50s skirt and top.

Barb: — Cindy's best friend, really into fashion. Her stylish look includes Capri pants and a necklace, which she gives to Cindy.

Judy: — Cindy's perky friend and the biggest fan of *At the Bandstand*. Dressed similarly to the girls on the show, including a scarf tied around her neck, which she gives to Cindy.

Peggy: — Cindy's tough friend. She's a tomboy, wearing jeans and a cardigan sweater, which she gives to Cindy.

Laverne: — Cindy's quirky friend. Looks like a nerd, acts like an airhead. Wears a plaid shirt and cat-eye glasses, plus a lucky ring, which she gives to Cindy.

*Darlene Worthington: — A spoiled Daddy's girl. Self-absorbed and entitled. '50s party dress.

*Miss Maisie Skippypaws: — Darlene's sidekick cat. Speaks in expressive feline noises, sings in English. Dressed in a fuzzy sweater and skirt with a pet collar around her neck and a cat ear headband in her hair.

Bandstand Kids: — The featured performers on *At the Bandstand*. Great singers and dancers uniformly dressed—girls in poodle skirts with matching tops and neck scarves, boys in dress slacks and sweater vests or cardigans. Any number of boys and girls may be added to the ensemble. Named characters include:

Girls:	Boys:
Betty Jo Riley	Brock McGreggor
Janice Hopkins	Carl St. Clair
Evelyn Finklestein	Michael Miller
Patty Pokowski	Mark Miller (*not twins*)

*Johnny James: — The most popular of all the Bandstand Kids. A dreamy crooner. Dressed like the other boys on the show.

Wanda Jean Hannigan: — Was a Bandstand Kid until a recent injury put her on crutches. She's outgoing, the life of the party. Wears a '50s outfit with one leg bandaged or in a cast.

Mr. Worthington: — Darlene's father and corporate sponsor of *At the Bandstand*. He wears a stuffy businessman's suit.

Optional Roles

Camera Operator: — Pretends to film the show with a fake TV camera on a wheeled tripod. Wears slacks and a pullover sweater.

Cue Card Holder: — Kneels while holding cue cards down front or near the camera as it moves. Jeans with a polo shirt and jacket.

* denotes vocal soloist

Setting

There are three performance areas, used simultaneously for much of the show.

1. The *At the Bandstand* Studio Set (center stage) – Hang a stylized "At the Bandstand" sign above your choral risers or a configuration of dance platforms. Optionally, oversized vinyl records, music notes, or '50s graphics may decorate the set further.

2. Cindy's House (downstage left) – A '50s couch and retro TV set (made with a cardboard box) are all you need. Optional items may include a lamp at the side of the couch, additional seating or floor pillows, and a throw rug. If desired, cast members may remove this scenery after song #6.

3. Darlene's Room (downstage right) – Another TV and a place to sit and primp. This could be a vanity with a stool or chair (including the frame of a mirror to look through), and/or an overly girlish bed. If desired, cast members may remove this scenery after song #6.

Props

Handheld microphone – for Robin

Retro telephone – for Darlene

Hairbrush and mirror – for Darlene

Judges table and two chairs – brought on by
   cast members after song #6

Toothbrush and tube of toothpaste – for Michael and Mark

"Splish Splash Bath Products" sign – for Brock and Johnny

Bath brushes – for "Splish Splash" choreography

Staging and Choreography

There are three scenes in progress at the same time for much of this musical, so you have a choice!

Option 1 – Everyone's On: The actors in Cindy's House and Darlene's Room watch *At the Bandstand* on their TV sets, miming reactions and or/singing along with the show. The Bandstand Kids sing and perform every song as a number prepared for TV, and in between, silently get to places as Robin pantomimes hosting duties.

Option 2 – Lights Out: Even without stage lights that come up and down on each scene, you can create the same effect by having actors freeze until their next feature.

Choreography notes are included above the music for each song. Use them as they appear or consider them only suggestions, designing your own creative movement.

About the Recording

At the Bandstand! was recorded by Tim Hayden at Ned's Place Recording Studio in Nashville, TN. Additional piano recordings were played by Sally K. Albrecht, and the project was mixed by Kent Heckman at Red Rock Recording in Saylorsburg, PA.

Performers include: Marisa Davila, Mallory Egly, Timothy Griffith, Lucy Hames, Faith Kennedy, Jaeden Kennedy, Hannah McGinley, Finn Pope, Michael Pope, Noah Pope, Anna Grace Stewart, Jasmine Swain, and Sarah Valley.

The **Enhanced SoundTrax CD** offers the following:

• Access to both Full-Performance and Accompaniment recordings (on your CD player).

• Downloadable PDF files of student pages and the full color cover/poster (on your computer). Purchase of this CD carries with it the right to display these images on an electronic blackboard in the classroom and/or on the school website.

Please visit our website and browse our Interactive Classroom Catalog at *alfred.com/classroom* to see sample pages, hear audio excerpts (where available), and discover more about all of Alfred's elementary musicals, programs, songbooks, classroom resources, and treble chorals.

About the Writers

Sally K. Albrecht

Sally K. Albrecht is a popular choral conductor, composer, and clinician, especially known for her work with choral movement. Sally received a B.A. from Rollins College with a double major in Music and Theater. From there she moved to the University of Miami, where she received both an M.A. in Drama and an M.M. in Accompanying. Sally has over 350 popular publications in print, including songbooks, musicals, and movement DVDs.

Jay Althouse

Jay Althouse received a B.S. in Music Education and an M.Ed. in Music from Indiana University of Pennsylvania, from which he received the school's Distinguished Alumni award. As a composer of choral music, Jay has over 500 works in print for choirs of all levels. His best-selling Alfred books include *The Complete Choral Warm-up Book, Accent on Composers, Ready to Read Music, 60 Music Quizzes,* and *One-Page Composer Bios.*

Andy Beck

Andy Beck is the Director of Choral Designs, Classroom, and Vocal Publications for Alfred Music. He received a bachelor's degree in Music Education from Ithaca College and a master's degree in Music Education from Northwest Missouri State University. A successful composer and arranger, Andy has authored several top-selling chorals, songbooks, and children's musicals, as well as co-written the highly regarded method, *Sing at First Sight, Foundations in Choral Sight-Singing, Volumes 1* and *2.*

Brian Fisher

Brian Fisher is a native of Pennsylvania, where he received a bachelor's degree in Quantitative Business Analysis from Penn State University. After several years as a bank auditor, he attended the State University of New York and became a teacher. Throughout his life, he has been active in music and theatre as an educator, director, and performer. Brian currently lives in North Carolina, where he teaches middle school.

Greg Gilpin

Greg Gilpin is originally from the "Show-Me" state of Missouri, and now resides in Indianapolis, IN. He is a graduate of Northwest Missouri State University with a bachelor's degree in Vocal Music Education, K-12. Greg is a well-known choral composer and arranger with hundreds of publications to his credit. He does numerous commissions throughout the year and special arranging projects for recorded works. He is also in demand as a conductor, clinician, studio producer, and performer.

1. AT THE BANDSTAND!

(Robin, Bandstand Kids, Cindy, Barb, Judy, Peggy, Laverne, Darlene, and Skippypaws)

Words and Music by
ANDY BECK

ROBIN: Greetings all you cats and kittens out there in TV land! It's time for the hippest, the heppest, the most happenin' dance party on the air. So gather 'round the tube as Splish Splash Bath Products proudly presents ... *AT THE BANDSTAND!*

Enter with excitement, taking places (ad lib. waving, high-fives, etc.)

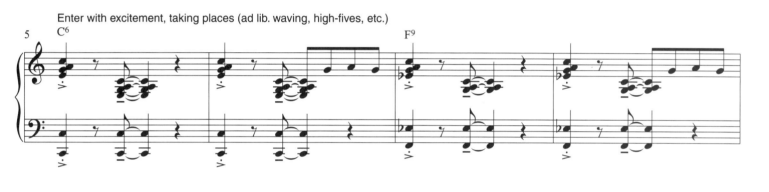

Strum guitar 8x, leaning over and back

13 BANDSTAND KIDS & ROBIN

*Swing "trumpet" (formed by gripping R thumb with L hand) up R, up L, down R, down L

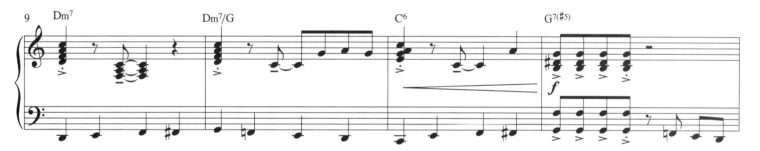

First we're gon - na rock, we'll rock a - round the clock at the band - stand!__

* Optional feet during "trumpet" swing: Walk R forward, L forward, R back, L back

© 2013 Alfred Music Publishing Co., Inc.
All Rights Reserved. Printed in USA.

39959

(The girls rush in to Cindy's House and gather around the TV.)

CINDY: Hurry girls, it's on!   **BARB:** I get the couch!   **JUDY:** Me, too.   **PEGGY:** Shh! I can't hear.

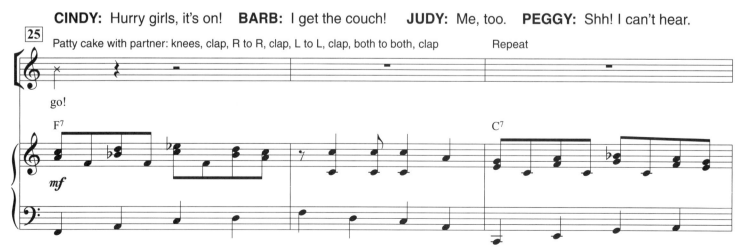

LAVERNE: What are we watching? **CINDY, BARB, JUDY & PEGGY:** Laverne!

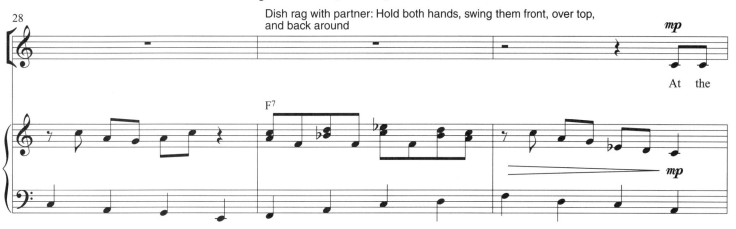

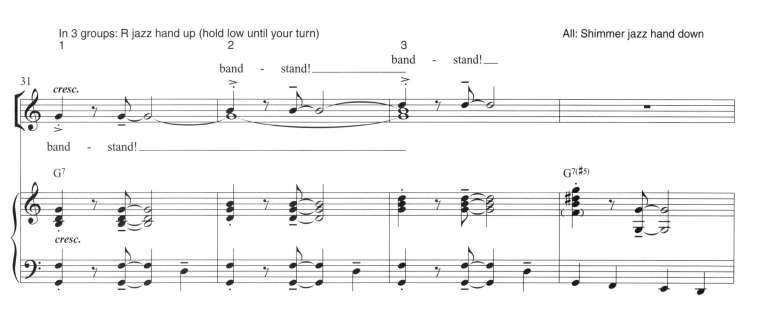

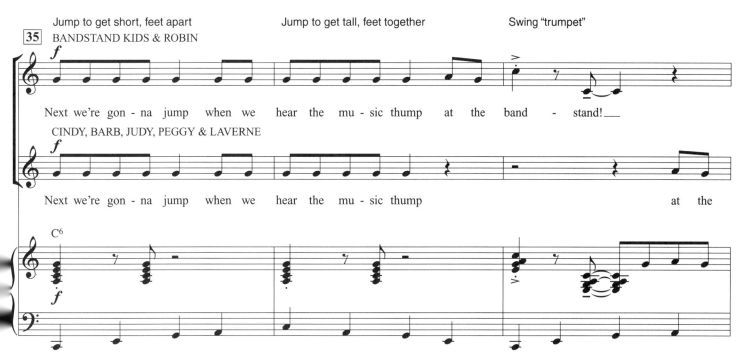

(A phone rings in Darlene's Room. Darlene enters with Miss Maisie Skippypaws (her cat) and answers the phone.)

DARLENE: Hello. ... Yes Daddy, I'm watching right now. ... Oh, really? A special announcement? ... I can hardly wait!

ROBIN: Thank you, thank you very much. This must be the most enthusiastic, most outrageous, and best-looking studio audience on television! *(pointing to a female audience member)* Especially you, little doll—I dig those bobby socks.

KIDS: *(getting him back on track)* Robin!

ROBIN: Let's kick off tonight's show by meeting our featured Bandstand Kids!

(The Kids applaud and cheer.)

ROBIN: First up—she's America's sweetheart, and a black belt in Tae Kwon Do … Betty Jo Riley!

(As Robin introduces each Kid, they run downstage and wave.)

BETTY JO: I break wood, not hearts!

CINDY: *(commenting on the show)* She seems nice.

ROBIN: Next—our resident motor head, and a drag race champion … Brock McGreggor!

BROCK: *(cheerfully)* I failed my driver's test twelve times!

PEGGY: That's better than you, Laverne.

LAVERNE: Hey!

ROBIN: She's the girl next door … for real, she's my neighbor … Janice Hopkins!

JANICE: *(smiling)* My mom says we should move.

JUDY: *(talking to the TV)* Move to my street, Janice!

ROBIN: This guy's the quarterback of the football team, and vice-president of the knitting club … Carl St. Clair!

CARL: *(bragging)* I made this sweater myself.

BARB: Is that cashmere?

ROBIN: A world-class yodeler, and three-time winner of the hog calling contest at the county fair … Evelyn Finklestein!

EVELYN: *(yodels)* Oh-de-lay-ee, oh-de-lay-ee, oh-de-lay-ee hoo! *(calls)* Suey!

SKIPPYPAWS: Meow.

DARLENE: Quiet down, Skippypaws.

ROBIN: Our very own dynamic duo … I can hardly tell them apart ... the Miller twins!

MICHAEL: *(not amused)* We look nothing alike.

MARK: *(confused)* We're not even related.

LAVERNE: *(clueless)* It's like I'm seeing double.

ROBIN: *At the Bandstand's* dance captain, and resident comedienne … Patty Pokowski!

PATTY: *(performing)* How many TV show hosts does it take to change a light bulb? …

ROBIN: *(interrupting)* … And everyone's favorite heartthrob, a crooner with a voice of gold and eyes of blue … it's Jumpin' Johnny James!

JOHNNY: *(with a wink)* Hi.

(Cindy, Barb, Judy, Peggy, and Laverne go crazy for Johnny. Cheering, screaming, swooning, etc.)

BARB: Be still my heart.

CINDY: He's the most!

ROBIN: Now it's time to board the train to Coolsville, and get this show on the road. What d'ya say, kids?

(The Kids applaud and cheer.)

ROBIN: But first, you're watching *At the Bandstand*, and I'm your host … Rockin' Robin!

2. ROCKIN' ROBIN

(Robin and Bandstand Kids)

Arranged by
ANDY BECK

Words and Music by
JIMMIE THOMAS

© 2013 by Alfred Music Publishing Co., Inc.
All Rights Reserved. Printed in USA.

39959

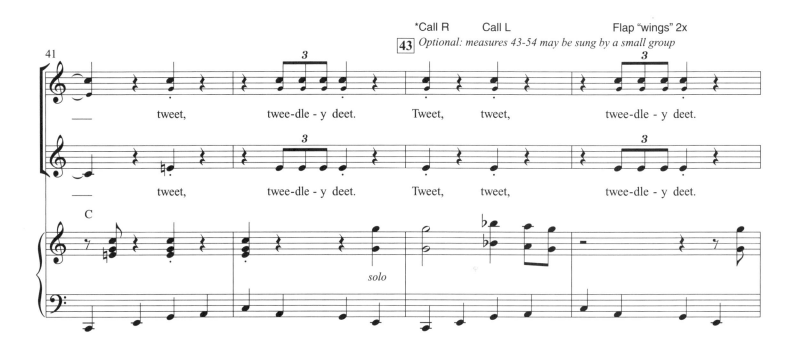

* Optional: Feature couples in a fancy swing dance break

ROBIN:	What a blast! You Bandstand Kids sure know how to rock!
KIDS:	*(ad lib.)* Thanks, Robin. You know it. Back at ya, daddy-o!
ROBIN:	*(to camera)* And there's a lot more of that to come, including a special announcement for our viewers at home.
JUDY:	Neat-o! I wonder what it is.
PEGGY:	Don't keep us in suspense, Robin.
ROBIN:	But before we get to all that, let's bring out the last member of our cast. This little lady's a prima ballerina at Miss Vicky's School of Dance, and everyone's favorite roller-skating waitress … Wanda Jean Hannigan!

(Wanda enters, on crutches. The Kids applaud.)

WANDA:	*(dejected)* Hey, everyone.
CINDY:	Oh, no! That's Johnny's partner.
ROBIN:	Gosh Wanda, looks like you've suffered an unfortunate mishap. Can you give us the scoop?
WANDA:	Well, I was working the lunch shift over at Bob's Burger Palace on Rt. 55, delivering an extra large order of big burgers with a side of Bob's cheesy fries.
LAVERNE:	Mmm, Bob's cheesy fries.
WANDA:	So just as I was picking up some speed, the new girl, Polly Sue, spilled her tray of chocolate malts. Now normally, I can maneuver on a pair of roller skates like nobody's business, but let me tell you, when my wheels hit that puddle of chocolate syrup and ice cream, I was a goner!
ROBIN:	Ooo, bummer.

WANDA: Yeah, I really wiped out. Like … splatsville!

DARLENE: What a klutz.

SKIPPYPAWS: *(laughing)* Sss.

ROBIN: So what's the story, morning glory? How long do you expect to be on those crutches?

WANDA: Dr. Goldberg said it'll be ten weeks 'til I can put on my dancing shoes and return to the show.

ROBIN: Tough break, kid.

WANDA: Yeah, it's no fun being on these crutches. But the insurance settlement is super swell!

CINDY: I wonder who will dance with Johnny.

BARB: *(teasing)* Bet'cha wish it were you, don't ya, Cindy?

CINDY: Who wouldn't?

ROBIN: Listen up, ladies—now that Wanda's out, Johnny needs a new partner. Isn't that right, Johnny?

JOHNNY: *(moving downstage)* That's right, Robin. Goin' stag is a drag!

3. SAVE THE LAST DANCE FOR ME

(Johnny and Bandstand Kids)

Arranged by
JAY ALTHOUSE

Music by **DOC POMUS**
Lyrics by **MORT SHUMAN**

CINDY: I think Johnny's gonna sing!

JUDY: Oh, I hope he'll sing!

DARLENE: Finally, something good, Skippypaws.

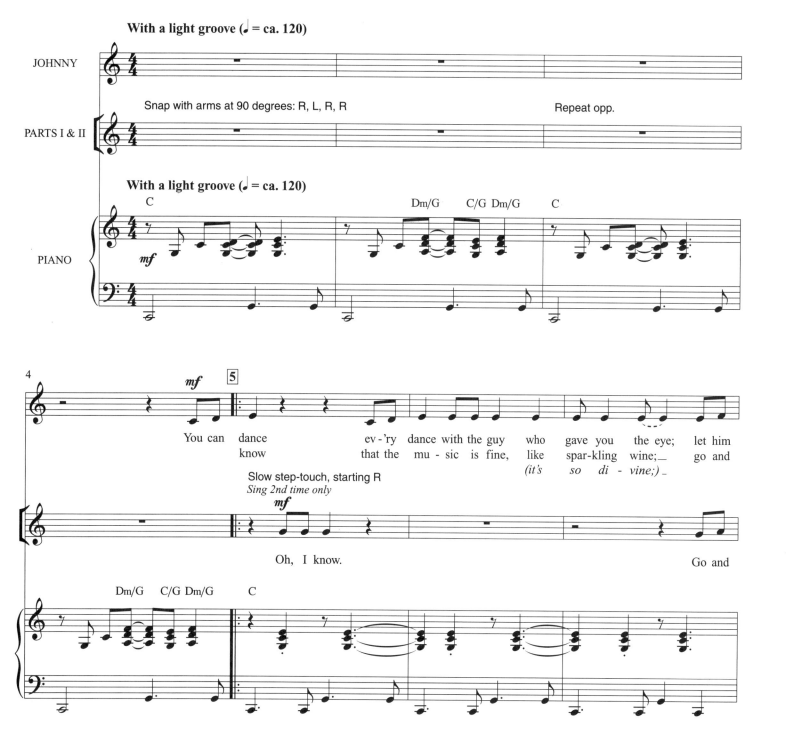

© 1960 (Renewed) Unichappell Music Inc.
This Arrangement © 2013 Alfred Music Publishing Co., Inc.
All Rights Reserved.   Printed in USA.

* Shimmer R jazz hand out to R, shimmer L jazz hand at tummy, leaning R, L, R, and tall
Feet: step R, together, R, together

LAVERNE: *(enthralled)* I'm on Cloud Nine!

BARB: In Seventh Heaven.

CINDY: He's soooo dreamy.

ROBIN: That's the stuff, Johnny. Just listen to the ladies swoon!

(Bandstand Kids girls swoon on cue.)

ROBIN: And that brings us to our big announcement, folks.

DARLENE: Here it comes, Skippypaws. Just like Daddy said.

ROBIN: *At the Bandstand* and Splish Splash Bath Products proudly present the Shake, Rattle and Roll Dance-Off! *(addressing the Bandstand Kids)* Tell us the rules, Kids.

JANICE: Participants must be girls between the ages of 12 and 18.

CARL: No previous dance experience necessary.

PATTY: Contestants should be no taller than Johnny, which is about ... *(looking at Johnny and gesturing)* this tall.

EVELYN: Soprano voices preferred. But altos are fine, too.

MICHAEL: Parties affiliated with *At the Bandstand*, or this television station, are not eligible to compete.

MARK: Parties affiliated with Splish Splash Bath Products are encouraged to!

BETTY JO: *At the Bandstand* is not responsible for dance injuries, hairdo mishaps, or scuffed saddle shoes.

BROCK: Winner must be able to cut eighth period on Wednesdays for practice.

ROBIN: So there ya have it kids, YOU could be the next Bandstand Kid, and dance with our very own Jumpin' Johnny!

(Cindy, Barb, Judy, Peggy, and Laverne cheer and applaud the great news.)

BARB: Can you believe it!?

JUDY: A chance to be a Bandstand Kid.

PEGGY: And dance with Johnny.

CINDY: It's a dream come true!

LAVERNE: Which one's Johnny?

CINDY: Laverne! He's only the niftiest, neatest, nicest boy there is.

JUDY: Not to mention the best singer and dancer on the show!

CINDY: He's an angel to me.

4. JOHNNY ANGEL

(Cindy, Barb, Judy, Peggy, and Laverne) *

Arranged by
JAY ALTHOUSE

Words by **LYN DUDDY**
Music by **LEE POCKRISS**

* Optional - The Bandstand Kids girls may perform this song as well, from center stage, as if a number on the show.

© 1962 (Renewed) EMILY MUSIC COMPANY and IVANHOE MUSIC
This Arrangement © 2013 EMILY MUSIC COMPANY and IVANHOE MUSIC
All Rights Reserved. Printed in USA.

PEGGY: *(pointing to the TV)* The show's back on!

ROBIN: … and our Shake, Rattle and Roll Dance-Off begins soon! So put the kibosh on what you're doin', get yourself dolled up, and boogie on down to the studio.

LAVERNE: Cindy, you have to try out.

CINDY: Me? Why?

JUDY: You're the best dancer. Everybody knows that!

CINDY: You really think so?

BARB: Of course. We all saw you at the sock hop.

CINDY: But, I …

PEGGY: Don't have a cow. You're going.

LAVERNE: And we're coming with you!

(Judy, Barb, and Peggy ad lib. agreement and excitement.)

ROBIN: Now it's time to introduce our contest judges. Starting with *At the Bandstand's* wobbly waitress, Wanda Jean Hannigan.

(The Bandstand Kids applaud enthusiastically for Wanda.)

WANDA: *(waving)* Hello again, everybody.

JUDY: I hope we get to meet her!

BARB: I hope Cindy gets to take her place.

ROBIN: And the owner and CEO of Splish Splash Bath Products, Raymond C. Worthington, III.

(The Bandstand Kids applaud politely for Worthington.)

WORTHINGTON: It's a pleasure to be here, Robin. And may the best girl win!

DARLENE: I know I will.

SKIPPYPAWS: *(agreeing)* Meow, purr.

DARLENE: That's right, Skippypaws.

JUDY: Do you realize who that is?

CINDY: Who?

JUDY: That's Darlene Worthington's father.

LAVERNE: Who's that?

PEGGY: You know. The rich girl with that "Skippypaws" cat.

CINDY: Do you think SHE'D show up for something like this?

BARB: Let's hope not!

5. SH-BOOM

(Darlene, Skippypaws, and Bandstand Kids)

Arranged by
ANDY BECK

Words and Music by **JAMES KEYES,**
CLAUDE FEASTER, CARL FEASTER,
FLOYD McRAE, *and* **JAMES EDWARDS**

DARLENE: Well, Miss Maisie Skippypaws, looks like I've got a competition to enter.

SKIPPYPAWS: Meow?

DARLENE: Of course you can come along. After all, I want you to be there when I win that dance-off and make Johnny my own.

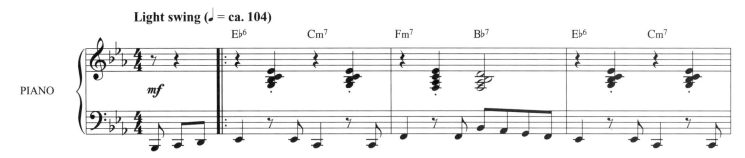

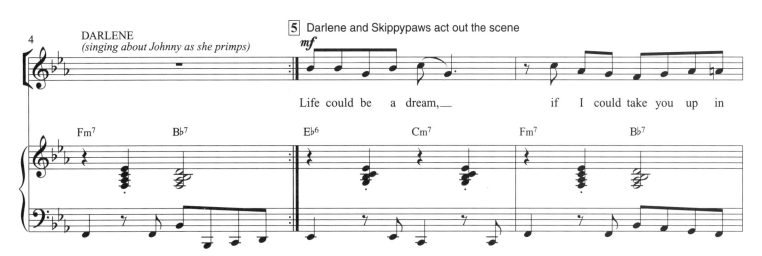

© 1954 (Renewed) UNICHAPPELL MUSIC INC.
This Arrangement © 2013 UNICHAPPELL MUSIC INC.
All Rights Reserved. Printed in USA.

(Action begins again at the Bandstand show.)

ROBIN: And now back to our terrific Bandstand Kids!
Bandstand Kids move into kickline formation and raise arms to neighbors' backs

46

CINDY: Robin said to get dolled up. I can't go like this.

JUDY: What do you mean, Cindy? You look nice.

CINDY: I want to look PERFECT.

BARB: Here, put on my necklace. It really matches your outfit.

PEGGY: And take my cardigan.

JUDY: Tie this scarf in your hair. It's just right!

LAVERNE: Wanna wear my lucky ring? I had it on when I aced that geometry test.

PEGGY: You got a C, Einstein.

LAVERNE: *(proudly)* I know!

(They huddle around Cindy, helping her dress. When they finish, Cindy steps out and does a twirl.)

CINDY: How do I look?

BARB: Beautiful!

PEGGY: Like a winner.

JUDY: Johnny will love it.

(The girls exit stage left, headed to the show.)

ROBIN: … but before the dance-off begins, a word from our sponsor.

(The Bandstand Kids overact as they perform the stylized commercial.)

EVELYN: Gosh Patty, your hair sure does glisten in the sunlight!

39959

BETTY JO: Yeah. What's the secret behind those shiny locks?

PATTY: Thanks, girls. Why, it must be my new Ultra-Shine Shampoo, with luscious lathering lotion.

(Brock and Johnny hold up an official logo sign as the group responds in unison.)

KIDS: … by Splish Splash Bath Products!

MARK: *(holding a toothbrush)* Aw nuts, looks like I've run outta toothpaste. How will I ever get Patty to notice my smile?

MICHAEL: *(handing Mark a tube)* Here, try my Minty Mouth Foaming Toothpaste. It's how I keep THESE pearly whites bright.

(Brock and Johnny hold the sign up again.)

KIDS: … by Splish Splash Bath Products!

CARL: *(dancing awkwardly with Janice, as if at a prom)* I don't think I've ever smelled a sweeter perfume than yours, Janice. What is that terrific floral scent?

JANICE: *(flattered)* Oh, Carl. You must be referring to my Buds to Suds Bath Soap, now available in five fragrances.

(Brock and Johnny hold the sign up once more.)

KIDS: … by Splish Splash Bath Products!

6. SPLISH SPLASH

(Bandstand Kids)

Arranged by
JAY ALTHOUSE

Words and Music by
BOBBY DARIN *and* **JEAN MURRAY**

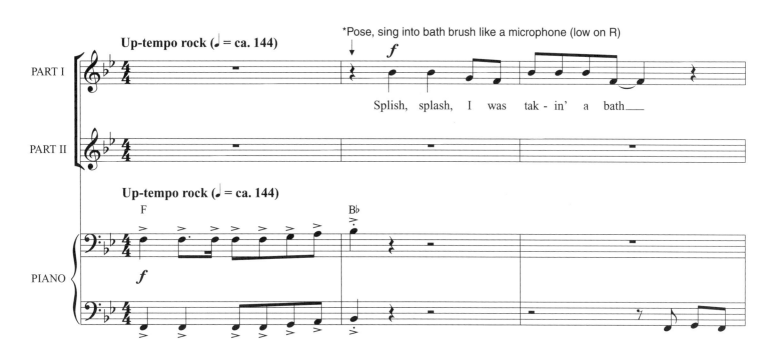

* Hold a prop bath brush in your R hand for this song

© 1958 (Renewed) EMI UNART MUSIC CATALOG INC., BUG MUSIC-TRIO MUSIC CO., INC., and ALLEY MUSIC CORP.
Exclusive Print Rights for EMI UNART CATALOG INC. Administered by ALFRED PUBLISHING CO., INC.
This Arrangement © 2013 EMI UNART CATALOG INC., BUG MUSIC-TRIO MUSIC CO., INC., and ALLEY MUSIC CORP.
All Rights Reserved. Printed in USA.

ROBIN: Thank you, Kids! And thank YOU, Splish Splash Bath Products. Don't touch that dial folks, the dance-off is next after a quick word from some of our other, *(to Worthington)* less important, sponsors. *(after a beat, off camera)* Okay, we've got three minutes to get set people. Let's move!

(During the next lines, the cast and/or stage crew prepares for the competition, removing furniture from Darlene's room and Cindy's house, and setting up a judges table with two chairs. At some point, Worthington and Wanda take their seats at the table. But first, the girls enter, an excited gaggle.)

JUDY: We're here! We're really here!

BARB: Can you believe it?

PEGGY: Somebody pinch me.

(Laverne pinches Peggy.)

PEGGY: Ouch! It's just an expression, Laverne.

LAVERNE: Sorry.

CINDY: Look! Robin is coming over here!

ROBIN: Hey, what's buzzin', cousin? Are you girls dancing in the competition?

BARB: *(pointing at Cindy)* She is.

ROBIN: *(addressing Cindy)* And what's your name, doll?

JUDY: *(interrupting before Cindy can answer, talking fast and shaking Robin's hand the whole time)* That's Cindy Sullivan, she's our friend, we watch your show every week, I can't believe I'm actually meeting you, I'm Judy, I'm your biggest fan!!

ROBIN: It's a kick to meet you, Judy. Now, how 'bout givin' me my hand back?

PEGGY: *(stepping in to pull them apart)* Don't mind her, she doesn't get out much.

ROBIN: Nice of you to make an exception for me. Good luck, Cindy. Enjoy the show, girls. *(He walks away.)*

JUDY: *(swooning)* I think I'm gonna faint!

LAVERNE: Just relax and breathe. *(demonstrating a breathing exercise)* In and out … in and out …

(The girls huddle around Judy. Darlene and Skippypaws enter and cross to the judges table.)

DARLENE: Hello, Daddy.

WORTHINGTON: Hello, kitten. So glad you made it.

SKIPPYPAWS: Meow.

WORTHINGTON: *(baby talk)* Aw, Miss Maisie Skippypaws.

SKIPPYPAWS: *(hissing)* Hhhh.

DARLENE: *(privately)* Is all of this really necessary, Daddy? Do I actually have to audition?

WORTHINGTON: It's just a formality, sweetheart. Play along.

ROBIN: Here we go, gang. We're back in three, two, *(gestures one)*. Welcome back, home viewers! Do you know what time it is?

KIDS: What time is it, Robin?

ROBIN: It's time to shake, …

KIDS: Shake!

ROBIN: rattle, …

KIDS: Rattle!

ROBIN: and ROLL!

KIDS: ROLL!

ROBIN: Let's meet our contestants. First up, a little lady who watches the show every week … Cindy Sullivan!

(Everyone cheers and applauds enthusiastically, especially Cindy's friends.)

PEGGY: *(getting carried away)* Let 'em have it, Sully!

ROBIN: And contestant number two, a girl whose closest friend is feline … Darlene Worthington.

(Everyone applauds politely.)

ROBIN: Okay, take your places everyone. And away we go!

7. SHAKE, RATTLE AND ROLL

(All)

Arranged, with new Words and Music, by
SALLY K. ALBRECHT

Words and Music by
CHARLES E. CALHOUN

1st time - **ROBIN:** You're first, Cindy. The Kids'll teach you the moves!
2nd time - **ROBIN:** You're up, Darlene. Show us what'cha got!
3rd time - **ROBIN:** All together now. Give it all ya got!

1st time - PART I *only (as Cindy learns the dance)*
2nd time - PART II *only (as Darlene learns the dance)*
3rd time - *Sing both parts (all dance)*

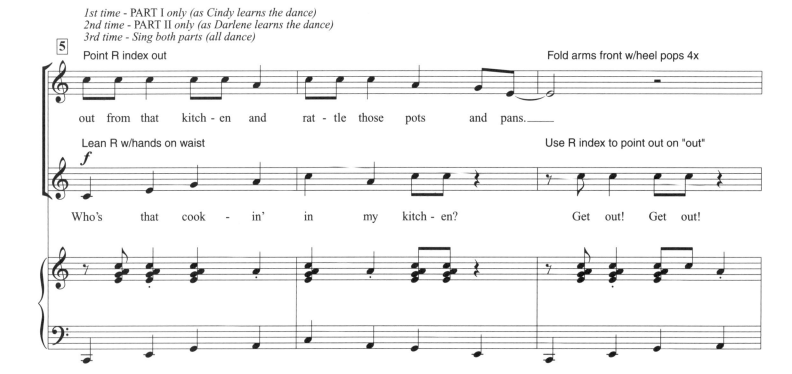

© 1954 (Renewed) UNICHAPPELL MUSIC INC. and MIJAC MUSIC
This Arrangement © 2013 UNICHAPPELL MUSIC INC. and MIJAC MUSIC
All Rights Reserved. Printed in USA.

ROBIN: Way to go, girls! You nearly blew the top off this joint. Now let's see what the judges have to say. Mr. Worthington?

WORTHINGTON: Well Robin, I think it's obvious—Darlene was born to be a Bandstand Kid!

(Everyone reacts with whispers.)

ROBIN: Okay. *(sarcastically)* Thank you for that … fair and impartial vote. And who do you pick, Wanda?

WANDA: I'm voting for Cindy. She's the best dancer.

(More reactions.)

ROBIN: *(thrown off a bit)* Um, looks like we've got a tie, folks. I'm not sure how to handle this.

PEGGY: I'll choose the winner!

BARB: Let us decide.

DARLENE: That's not fair!

WORTHINGTON: Perhaps Skippypaws should choose!

SKIPPYPAWS: *(agreeing)* Meow.

LAVERNE: Cats can't vote!

JUDY: Let the home viewers call in.

JOHNNY: Well, she'll be my dance partner. Can I pick?

ROBIN: That's actually not a bad idea. What do you think, Kids? Should we let Johnny decide?

KIDS: *(ad lib.)* Yes! Of course. Sure! You bet. Why not?

ROBIN: Alrighty then. Looks like it's up to you, Johnny. Whaddaya say?

(Johnny thinks for a moment and then breaks into song, the staging of which makes it clear that he has chosen Cindy.)

8. GREAT BALLS OF FIRE

(Johnny and Bandstand Kids)

Arranged by
GREG GILPIN

Words and Music by
OTIS BLACKWELL
and **JACK HAMMER**

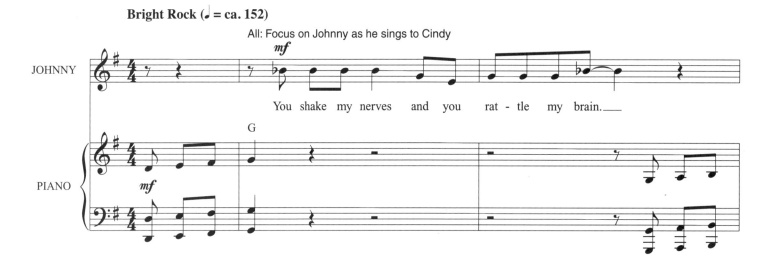

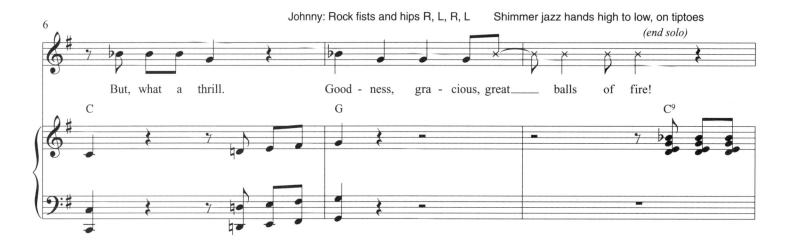

© 1957 (Renewed) UNICHAPPELL MUSIC INC., CHAPPELL & CO., INC.,
MIJAC MUSIC, and MYSTICAL LIGHT MUSIC
This Arrangement © 2013 UNICHAPPELL MUSIC INC., CHAPPELL & CO., INC.,
MIJAC MUSIC, and MYSTICAL LIGHT MUSIC
All Rights Reserved. Printed in USA.

39959

ROBIN: We have a winner. Let's hear it for our newest *At the Bandstand* Kid … Cindy Sullivan!

(Everyone cheers and applauds as Cindy moves center.)

ROBIN: Congratulations, kiddo! Do you have anything you wanna say?

CINDY: Wow, what an honor! This is just so cool. I'd like to thank my friends Judy, Barb, Peggy, and Laverne.

(Judy, Barb, Peggy, and Laverne cheer.)

CINDY: And I promise to do my very best to fill Wanda's shoes. Her dancing shoes, that is!

ROBIN: Let's introduce you to your Bandstand partner. Johnny, come over here and say hello.

JOHNNY: Hey, Cindy. Your dancing was really swell.

CINDY: Aw, gee. Thanks.

DARLENE: Ew! Can you believe this, Skippypaws?

SKIPPYPAWS: *(shrugging)* Meow.

ROBIN: And we haven't forgotten about you, Darlene. As first runner-up, you're going home with a year's supply of Splish Splash Bath Products!

DARLENE: *(disgusted)* Oh please! We don't actually use that stuff!

WORTHINGTON: Darlene!

DARLENE: It's true, Daddy. I wouldn't even use it on Skippypaws.

SKIPPYPAWS: *(agreeing)* Meow.

ROBIN: *(trying to get the show back on track)* Let's thank our judges, Wanda Jean Hannigan and Raymond C. Worthington!

WORTHINGTON: This is the last time you'll ever see me at this rinky-dink show. I'm officially withdrawing my sponsorship. And without me, you'll be off the air in a week!

ALL: *(ad lib.)* Oh no! What'll we do? That's horrible. No show?

WANDA: Don't count on it, Mr. Worthington. I have a new sponsor.

WORTHINGTON: Who?

WANDA: Me.

ROBIN: *(genuine)* Oh, that's very nice, Wanda, but this is an expensive operation. Where will you get the money?

WANDA: Remember that generous insurance settlement I mentioned from Bob's Burger Palace?

KIDS: Yeah?

WANDA: Well, how does this sound? … *At the Bandstand*, presented by Wanda's Burger Palace.

ROBIN: *(delighted)* Sounds like we have a new sponsor!

(Everyone applauds and cheers as Robin and Wanda shake hands.)

9. AT THE BANDSTAND! FINALE

(All)

Words and Music by
ANDY BECK

ROBIN: Well, that does it for this week's episode. I'm your host, Rockin' Robin, and

that's the word from the bird. See you next week on ...   **ALL:** *AT THE BANDSTAND!*

Repeat choreography as in song #1
9 ROBIN, BANDSTAND KIDS, WANDA, CINDY, BARB, JUDY, PEGGY & LAVERNE

First we're gon-na rock, we'll rock a-round the clock at the band - stand!__

© 2013 by Alfred Music Publishing Co., Inc.
All Rights Reserved. Printed in USA.

DARLENE: I've had enough of this. Take me home, Daddy.

WORTHINGTON: Whatever you say, sweetheart. I'll bring the car around. *(He exits.)*

DARLENE: (*starts to exit, then turns back*) Come along, Skippypaws.

At the

(*Skippypaws looks at Darlene, looks at the kids, looks back at Darlene and finally turns her nose in the air, indicating that she is not leaving.*)

DARLENE: (*exasperated*)
Oh, never mind! (*She exits.*)

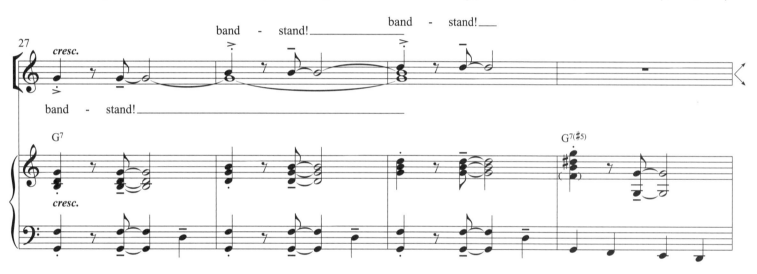

band - stand! _____ band - stand! ____

band - stand! _____

BANDSTAND KIDS, CINDY & ROBIN

Next we're gon - na jump when we hear the mu - sic thump at the band - stand! ____

SKIPPYPAWS, WANDA, BARB, JUDY, PEGGY & LAVERNE

Next we're gon - na jump when we hear the mu - sic thump at the

39959

BARB: *(thrilled)* What a day!

JUDY: *(star-struck)* Rockin' Robin touched my hand.

PEGGY: And you'll never wash it again!

LAVERNE: Too bad we missed our favorite TV show. **BARB, JUDY & PEGGY:** Laverne!

10. AT THE BANDSTAND! BOWS

(All)

Words and Music by
ANDY BECK

© 2013 by Alfred Music Publishing Co., Inc.
All Rights Reserved.   Printed in USA.

Repeat choreography as in song #1